Why I
Believe the Bible
Is the Word of God

D0901213

Phyllis Robinson

WHY I BELIEVE THE BIBLE IS THE WORD OF GOD

Why I Believe the Bible Is the Word of God By Phyllis Robinson

Cover design: Don Jones, www.brotherjones.com

All Scripture quotations are from the New King James Version of the Bible. Copyright © 1979, 1980, 1982 by Thomas Nelson, Inc., publishers, and from the New International Version.

Sixth Printing 2011

ISBN 1-930027-83-4
Library of Congress catalog card number: 2002115427

Printed in the United States of America

Dedication

Tim, Karen, Jenny, Troy,
Daniel and Michael.

You were on my mind when I began
writing this book. It is my legacy to you.

Contents

Acknowledgments

Ruth Hallett
Grace Tullio
Tovey Talley
Rich Williams
Al and Ruth Roberts
Pastor Mark Merrill

You helped and encouraged! Thank you!

Dear Husband Ron,

Your love translates into help!

❧✦

Introduction

Why I Believe the
Bible Is the Word of God

Rachael Scott, the young girl who was shot to death at Columbine high school, had the habit of carrying her Bible to school. When the troubled young man pointed his gun at her and asked if she believed in God, she could not deny her faith knowing it might cost her life. Her faith in God was made strong through the reading of His Word. The Bible itself says, "Now faith comes by hearing and hearing by the Word of God." God made Himself real to her through His Word. She was confident that if she died she would be with the God she had come to love through the reading of His Word.

Heaven has many martyrs who were willing to die for their faith. Do we who call ourselves Christian believe in this book by blind faith? No. The Scripture itself tells us, "Be ready always to give an answer to every man that asks you a reason of the hope that is in you" (1 Peter 3:15). I began to seriously study the Bible at age thirteen. I met often with a group of teens for Bible study and prayer. I continued to study God's Word after graduation from Bible college and the ensuing years. Now I have grandchildren in their teens. When I am gone from this earth, will my six grandchildren know exactly what I believed and why? Will they have any reason to think they will ever see their grandmother again? We have lived very close to four of these children and have developed a strong emotional bond. Will they feel hopeless when I'm gone? I must give them the same hope that I had when my own mother left this earth—the hope, no, the confidence that I shall see her again. How can I feel confident? It is my goal that this book will answer these questions.

In the early 1900's my grandfather attended a men's Bible class in Rochester, New York. I have been told that he really wanted to believe, but one thing made him skeptical. It was the Bible teaching that one day Israel would once again become a nation. At that point in time, Israel was scattered among the nations of the earth. My grandfather could not imagine why the Jews would ever want to return to that desert. To his finite mind it would take a miracle to draw an entire nation that had been driven out almost three thousand years earlier to a land that had become nothing more than a desert. Mark Twain, who visited the Holy Land back in Grandpa's day, wrote that he saw nothing but sand and one Bedouin nomad on a camel.

We now have experienced the fulfillment of that prophecy in which God said to Ezekiel in chapter 11 verse 17:

Therefore say: "This is what the Sovereign LORD says: I will gather you from the nations and bring you back from the countries where you have been scattered, and I will give you back the land of Israel again."

There are other fulfilled prophecies I'd like to share before we get to Israel, the most fascinating of all. My list of reasons for believing is below:

- Fulfilled Old Testament Prophecies
- Archeological Discoveries
- Scientific Confirmation
- Prophecy Concerning Israel
- Prophecies Concerning Jesus
- Changed Lives

Chapter One

Fulfilled Prophecies

*L*et's start with some fulfilled prophecies that have been historically proven. There are more than two thousand in the Old Testament that have already been fulfilled. I'll just choose a few of my favorites. Some Bible scholars refer to the Bible as "His Story." History? Yes, but more importantly, God's story of His love for the human race—His love for you and for me. You may read the words and say, "The Bible is too difficult for me to understand. There are too many wars and too many genealogy lists." Obviously, God did not intend His people to simply *read* His words. One Hebrew scholar said that, correctly interpreted, the Hebrew tells us to not only read these words, but, also to "search as for fine gold!" Here is an awesome example. First Chronicles 1:1 gives the genealogies of Adam through Abraham. Boring? Maybe not! Here is the list: Adam, Seth, Enosh, Kenan, Mahalalel, Jared, Enoch, Methuselah, Lamech, Noah. Names and their meanings were very important to God and to His ancient people. For instance, Abraham's parents named him Abram, but God changed it later to Abraham because that meant "father of many nations." Since then he has been known as the great patriarch of the Jewish and Arab people.

Look at the meanings of the names of the people in Adam's genealogy and see if God might have been trying to communicate His love to us through these names. Communicate His love? Just watch. I will list the names in the order given in the Scripture and list the meaning of these names alongside:

Adam	Man
Seth	Appointed
Enosh	Mortal
Kenan	Sorrow
Mahalalel	Blessed God
Jared	Shall Come Down
Enoch	Teaching
Methuselah	His death shall bring
Lamech	Despairing
Noah	Comfort, rest

God's message of love to us: Man (is) appointed (to) mortal sorrow; (but) the Blessed God shall come down teaching (that) His death shall bring (the) despairing rest." Imagine that! God revealed that He had a plan from the beginning of time to redeem mankind. The "blessed God" did "come down" and through "His death" on the cross, purchased our eternal "comfort and rest." Little did the Jewish rabbis realize, as they laboriously copied the Hebrew Scriptures, the message they were bringing to us from God.

They were actually prophesying or foretelling the death of their Messiah! Amazing! (From the book *Dictionary of Old Testament Proper Names*, by Alfred Jones, Kregel Publications, 1990)

The Bible is the only religious book in the world that contains prophecies. That's because only the God of the Bible knows the future. In all of the writings of Buddha, Confucius, and Lao-tse, you will not find a single example of predicted prophecy.

For everything that was written in the past was written to teach us.

Romans 15:4

In the Koran there is one instance of a specific prophecy and that's Mohammed's self-fulfilling prophecy, that he would return to Mecca. This is quite different from the prophecy of Jesus, who said that he would return from the dead. One is easily fulfilled, and the other is impossible to any human. Do I believe Jesus actually rose from the dead? Yes. I will address that under number five of my list.

Think about recent so-called prophets. Jean Dixon falsely "prophesied" who would be candidates for major parties of presidential elections in '52, '56, and '60 and who would win. She missed everyone! The 1978 *National Enquirer* had 61 predictions of 10 leading "psychics" for the last half of 1978. They missed them all! Yet, the Bible contains over 2,000 specific, predictive prophecies that have already been fulfilled. There is one that I find particularly interesting. I like it because it took many hundreds of years to be fulfilled, which means it could not have been prophesied after the fact. It's the prophecy concerning the city of Tyre, found in the book of Ezekiel chapter 26.

When the city of Tyre was at its height, Ezekiel, God's prophet, declared that it would be destroyed, never to be rebuilt and never again to be inhabited. This is what he said:

And they shall destroy the walls of Tyre, and break down her towers: I will also scrape her dust from her, and make her like the top of a rock. It shall be like a place for the spreading of nets in the midst of the sea: for I have spoken it, says the Lord God...and they will lay your stones and your timber and your dust in the midst of the water...and I will make you like the top of a rock...you will be built up no more: for I the Lord have spoken it.
Ezekiel 26:4-5, 12-14

A few years after the writing of this prophecy, Nebuchadnezzar began attacking the city of Tyre. For thirteen years the city withstood the Babylonian army. Finally the walls of the city crumbled, killing most of the inhabitants. Thousands, however, fled to the sea by boat to form a new city on an island a half-mile out in the Mediterranean. But that fulfilled only a part of the prophecy! God had said the city would be scraped clean like the top of a rock. Two hundred and fifty years later most of the walls of Tyre still stood declaring that the prophecy had not been completely fulfilled. God had said that the stones and timber and dust would end up on the water. Any skeptic who came along during that period of time would have declared Ezekiel a false prophet and his God to be a liar! Then came along Alexander the Great, an unlikely servant of the Most High, yet God used him to bring about the continued fulfillment of His prophecy against Tyre.

When Alexander the Great found the new city of Tyre, he, along with his chief engineer, Diades, decided to build a half-mile long causeway out into the Mediterranean—a feat unheard of in his day! Was he driven by greed or by God? God's will was certainly being accomplished here. Charles Mercer in his book, *Alexander the Great*, describes it this way:

Mainland Tyre was leveled, and its rubble was carried to the construction site. Meanwhile, logs were dragged from the forests of Lebanon, and quarries were opened in the hills to supply stones for Diades' fabulous highway . . . Alexander himself carried stones on his back.

History tells us that they scraped the city itself to get everything they could to make this highway in order to destroy the new city of Tyre! Prophecy fulfilled, right? Not quite. It still had to become "like a place for the spreading of nets."

. . . before they spring into being I announce them to you.

Isaiah 42:9

In his book, *Why I Believe*, D.J. Kennedy tells of a couple from his church who visited the site of the ancient city of

Tyre. They returned with pictures of nets spread on the flat rock that once had been Tyre. "For I have spoken it says the Lord God" (Ezekiel 26:5). And to think that our Holy Bible contains over two thousand such historically accurate fulfilled prophecies! Doesn't this make you want to study this book and get to know the God of the Bible better?

Another very interesting prophecy from the book of Ezekiel concerns the country of Egypt. At one time, Egypt was the greatest nation in the world. It was the richest country on earth. Yet, in spite of this, Ezekiel 30:13 gives a surprising and unusual prophecy about her future, "There shall no longer be princes from the land of Egypt." Recently, Egypt has gone to a democratic form of government. Before that it had always been ruled by a prince. But, amazingly, during the nearly 2,500 hundred years between this prophecy and Egypt's change to a democracy, its princes were never Egyptian! Can you imagine anyone being president of the United States without being an American? History confirms the fulfillment of this prophecy. Constantine Volney wrote:

> Deprived 2,300 years ago of her natural proprietors, Egypt has seen her fertile fields successively prey to the Persians, the Macedonians, the Romans, the Greeks, the Arabs, the Georgians, and at length, the race of Tartars distinguished by the name of Ottoman Turks; the Mamelukes soon usurped the power and elected a leader.

After Volney's time, in the last century, Mohammed Ali (not the boxer) established the princedom again in Egypt. Would this thwart God's word to Ezekiel? Egypt had been 2,300 years without a prince. Not to worry—the prince was born in Macedonia. His father was an

Albanian. After this, Egypt was ruled by the French and the English. (*Skeptics Answered* by D.J. Kennedy).

Do you wonder why God's judgment fell on Tyre and Egypt? In both cases the inhabitants refused to worship God or believe His prophets. Does God care about the moral and spiritual condition of our country?

Billy Graham once said, "If God does not judge America for her sins, He will have to apologize for destroying Sodom and Gomorrah." The

ᗒᗕ

B—Basic
I—Instructions
B—Before
L—Leaving
E—Earth

Bible contains more than 1,500 predictions concerning cities and countries. There is a creator God who has spoken to us through His prophets and through His Son Jesus Christ. This is how He puts it in Hebrews chapter one: "In the past, God spoke to our forefathers through the prophets at many times and in various ways, but in these last days He has spoken to us by His Son. . . ." God is a holy and righteous God. In His Word He has established His principles for living. When we, as nations or individuals, refuse to listen to Him, we must pay the price for disobedience. Does God seem harsh? Think about this: if your child gets injured in an accident while drinking and driving against your rules, who deserves the consequence? Get to know God as your Father and His Word as your instructions for living.

※

Chapter Two

Archeology

They lay on their stomachs in the desert, sometimes with nothing more than a brush in their hands carefully flicking away the sand. Who are these people? Some of them are devout Christians who love the land of the Bible. Others are simply seeking to uncover treasures of antiquity. All are servants of our Most High God—some knowingly and some unknowingly. In recent years He has been using these archeologists to confirm His Word and to silence the skeptic.

During the last part of the nineteenth century when leading Christian scholars began to tear the Bible apart, there came a surge of archeology. Many archeologists were seeking to discredit the Bible. All failed.

Have you heard the Biblical story of Joseph, whose jealous brothers sold him into slavery in Egypt? Eventually, because of famine in the land, Joseph's entire family moved to Egypt where there was plenty of grain stored. Later, things took a turn for the worse for the Israelites, and they became slaves of the Egyptians. The Bible tells us that the Pharaoh made them build the cities of Pithom and Ramses. In the book of Exodus chapter 5, we read how they were forced to gather straw and finally how they were told to build the bricks without any straw.

When archeologists discovered the sites of Pithom and Ramses, they discovered they were built with mortar—something found nowhere else in Egypt. Now, here's the fun part. The lower layers were built of brick in which was stubble instead of straw. In the second and upper

layers were bricks made without straw!
Awesome! The more I dig, although not
in the sand as the
archeologists do,
the more affirma-
tions I find that the
Bible is indeed the

&c&

...the stones will cry out.
Luke 19:40

inspired Word of God. This reminds me
of another verse of Scripture: "And you
shall seek Me, and find Me, when you
shall search for Me with all your heart"
(Jeremiah 29:13). We evidently cannot be
casual in our pursuit of God.

Here is another interesting discov-
ery concerning Joseph. In Genesis 50:24-
26, we read:

> *Then Joseph said to his brothers, "I am*
> *about to die. But God will surely come*
> *to your aid and take you up out of this*
> *land to the land He promised on oath*
> *to Abraham, Isaac and Jacob." And*
> *Joseph made the sons of Israel swear an*
> *oath and said, "God will surely come*

to your aid, and then you must carry my bones up from this place." So Joseph died at the age of a hundred and ten. And after they embalmed him, he was placed in a coffin in Egypt.

In Joshua 24:32, we read how centuries later Joseph's bones were "buried at Shechem in the tract of land that Jacob bought.

In the late 1950's a tomb in Shechem was opened. This tomb had been revered for centuries as the burial place of Joseph. Inside was a body mummified according to Egyptian custom. The tomb also contained a sword of the type worn by Egyptian officials. Not only is finding an Egyptian mummy in Shechem interesting but so is the fact that the Israelites remained in Egypt for at least 300 years after Joseph's death. If I requested, on my deathbed, that my family make sure my bones were buried in Europe where my ancestors came from, how likely would that request be carried out 300 years later? (Especially if they had to carry my mummified body on foot across Europe for forty years!)

Ralph Muncaster, former skeptic, wrote in his booklet, "Is The Bible Really A Message from God?" that large quantities of grain were found inside Jericho—a highly unusual event for a city that had been conquered. The Bible explains that God commanded the Israelites to leave things untouched other than valuable metals to be placed in the treasury (Joshua 6:17-19).

Muncaster has made other interesting observations:

(1) Formerly, the early Hittites were thought to be nonexistent in Abraham's time. Now entire museums of Hittite artifacts exist.
(2) Cities including Sodom and Gomorrah were thought to be myths until archeology confirmed their existence.

(3) A receipt was discovered for a ration of oil, barley and other food to King Jehoiachin, who was in captivity in Babylon. This receipt lists Jehoiachin, the king in Judah, and his five sons as recipients of the issues of food. The Bible indicates that the king of Babylon brought Jehoiachin out of prison and gave him a daily allowance for the rest of his life (2 Kings 25:27-30). On a separate stone tablet written in the seventh year of Nebuchadnezzar, accounts of the fall of Jerusalem, the capture of Jehoiachin, and the appointment of a new king are recorded.

So far, all of these examples have come from the Old Testament. But, as Grant Jeffrey in his book *Signature of God*, points out:

The entire basis for the faith and hope of Christians depends on the truthfulness of the historical records of the New Testament. Our hope for heaven and salvation itself depends on the accuracy of the words of Jesus of Nazareth and the apostles as recorded in the pages of the New Testament manuscripts. . . . Fortunately, the continued archeological discoveries during the last century have provided an awesome amount of evidence that confirms the total reliability of the written documents that form the foundation of the Christian faith.

The great archeologist Sir William Ramsay, who devoted thirty years of his life trying to disprove the book of Acts, was converted to Christianity as a result of his findings. This sounds like a fulfillment of the prophecy Jesus made in Luke 19:40. The Pharisees tried to get Him to quiet His disciples. "I tell you," Jesus replied, "If they keep quiet, the stones will cry out." Surely the stones cried out to Sir William!

One of the greatest intellectual hindrances to accepting the writings of the New Testament has been that many skeptics thought there was too much lapse of time between the written accounts in the New Testament books and the actual events. However, recent discoveries prove that the Gospels were written within a few years of the events described. It is interesting to note that these same scholars readily accept the authenticity of Julius Caesar's *Gallic Wars* written 1,000 years after the events. The first existing manuscript of Homer's *Iliad* was written 500 years after the events.

According to Grant Jeffrey:

&ᔁ

Therefore I will make Samaria a heap of rubble...and lay bare her foundations.

Micah 1:6

Dr. John A. T. Robinson was a distinguished lecturer at Trinity College, Cambridge, who developed a reputation as a great scholar. He accepted the academic consensus universally held since 1900, that denied the disciples and Paul wrote the New Testament and concluded that it was written up to one hundred years after Christ. However, an article in *Time* magazine, March 21, 1977, reported that Robinson decided to personally investigate for himself the arguments behind this scholarly consensus against the New Testament's reliability because he realized that very little original research had been completed in this field in this century. He was shocked to discover that much of past scholarship against the New Testament was untenable because it was based on a 'tyranny of unexamined assumptions' and what he felt must have been an 'almost willful blindness.' To the amazement of his university colleagues, Robinson concluded that the apostles must have been the genuine writers of the New Testament books in the years prior to A.D. 64.

That would be only twenty-one years after the death and resurrection of Jesus Christ.

But what about Jesus? Was He the Christ—the Messiah? Was His birth miraculous? Was He resurrected from the dead? If I hang the hope of my eternal salvation on Him alone, I'd better have some answers! I'll put aside the temptation to deal with this now and go to the next category on my list: scientific confirmation.

Chapter Three

Scientific Confirmation

Ralph O. Muncaster in his booklet, "Science—Was the Bible Ahead of Its Time?" introduces this subject better than I could:

> The more the Bible is studied, the more surprising it becomes that people often think it is in conflict with science. Yet science's rejection of the Bible has become common only in the last hundred years. Great scientists of the past, including Newton, Kepler, and Galileo, were all avid readers and believers of the Bible.

The decline in a scientific belief in God can be traced to Darwin's theory of evolution, introduced in 1860. This alternative to creation, combined with the prevalent theory of an infinite universe, caused many scientists to turn away from God and the Bible. But even as early as 1916, Einstein's general relativity breakthrough contained ample evidence to refute evolution with pure mathematical probability. Only in recent years has general relativity been essentially "proven." (Einstein begrudgingly admitted the probability of a Creator.) Unfortunately, the world is slow to recognize the new scientific evidence supporting the Bible—and much outdated information is still in student text books. Scientific evidence of God is now increasing rapidly—and gradually the scientific world is becoming aware of many new breakthroughs.

As Patrick Glynn, a scholar and former atheist, explains in *God: The Evidence,* "Modern thinkers assumed that science would reveal the universe to be ever more random and mechanical; instead it has discovered unexpected new layers of intricate order that bespeak an almost unimaginably vast master design."

Physicist Paul Davies writes, "Through my scientific work I have come to believe more and more strongly that the physical universe is put together with an ingenuity so astonishing that I cannot accept it merely as a brute fact. There must, as it seems to me, be a deeper level of explanation."

And here is a quote from Fred Hoyle, astronomer: "Yet as biochemists discover more and more about the awesome complexity of life, it is apparent that the chances of it originating by accident are so minute that they can be completely ruled out. Life cannot have arisen by chance."

While it is reassuring to read the above quotes and those of many other modern scholars with great scientific minds, my own non-scientifically oriented mind was made up as a teenager when I learned how scientifically accurate the Bible is.

The Bible clearly states in Leviticus 17:11, "The life of the flesh is in the blood." For centuries, physicians practiced blood-letting in an attempt to rid the body of poison. Blood-letting was the cause of George Washington's death. Thankfully, in this regard, medical science has caught up with the Bible.

On the subject of blood, why did God instruct the children of Israel to circumcise the baby boys on the *eighth* day after birth (Genesis 17:12)? We can be quite certain that Moses had no knowledge of what we call vitamin K. Yet the medical profession now knows that vitamin K is necessary for the production of prothrombin, the body's blood-clotting substance. We also know that this substance is about 110 percent of normal on the *eighth* day! Furthermore, why did God institute this practice at all? "In 1954, in a vast study of 86,214 women in Boston, it was observed that cancer of the cervix in non-Jewish women was eight and one half times more frequent than in Jewish women. Why are Jewish women comparatively free of cervical cancer? Medical researchers now agree that this spectacular freedom results from the practice of circumcision in Jewish men—which God ordered Abraham to institute 4,000 years ago." (From the book, *None of These Diseases*, by S.I. McMillen, M.D.). More recent research has implicated the smegma bacillus, which can be carried in the foreskin of uncircumcised males and is a cancer-causing agent.

What about germs? As a young person I was amazed to read about the physician who was ostracized by the medical community when he tried to persuade them that deaths were caused by not practicing hand-washing between performing autopsies and doing pelvic exams. This poor man died in a mental institution. If only his colleagues had read and believed Numbers 19 where guidelines for washing are stressed in the handling of the dead, many lives could have been spared.

ॐॐ

The heavens declare the glory of God; the skies proclaim the work of his hands.

Psalm 19:1

Recently, while visiting an open house, we had an interesting conversation with the realtor who listed the house.

He told us that a realtor's worst nightmare is that the inspectors will find mold on the premises. Current research is showing that mold is extremely dangerous to human health, especially to the brain. Entire schools have had to be evacuated because of stachybotrys (black mold), and one friend in Texas had to vacate his house with just the clothing on his back when black mold was discovered. This is one more reason why I believe the Bible is the Word of God. It warned us of the danger of mold in Leviticus 14:35-45:

> . . . *the owner of the house must go and tell the priest, "I have seen something that looks like mildew in my house." The priest is to order the house to be emptied before he goes in to examine the mildew...if the mildew has spread on the walls, he is to order that the contaminated stones be torn out and thrown into an unclean place outside the town...it must be torn*

down—its stones, timbers and all the plaster taken out of the town to an unclean place.

An article in *USA Weekend*, August 2000, lists some of the possible effects of mold on human health: headaches, congestion, ear infections, shortness of breath, spontaneous nosebleeds, memory problems, and chest pains. Experts in a documentary on Channel 6 in Tulsa, Oklahoma, report these symptoms from mold exposure: allergic rhinitis, fever, severe skin rashes, immune system suppression, malaise, lung infections, ear infections, shortness of breath, heart racing, and others. Here's what former biology teacher Martha Bryant has to say about stachybotrys: "It produces a toxin that compromises your immune system, so diseases like cancer can move in. The toxin also affects your memory. It can kill your neurons, and the rate at which it kills them depends on how you react to the toxin." Other molds implicated are *cladisporium*, *aspergillus*, *penicillium*, and *altineria*. Whole books have been written on how up to date is this very old book, the Holy Bible!

In Leviticus 25:4, God instructed the Israelites to give the land a rest every seven years. He also taught them to bury the refuse (composting). Both practices give important minerals back into the soil. Until 1988, the FDA annually published the mineral content of fruits and vegetables grown in our country. Each food was broken down into an ash and the contents analyzed. I have been told that in 1988 it took one bushel of corn to equal the nutrients in one ear of corn grown in the 1930's!

A study done at Rutgers University in the 1940's showed the difference in mineral content in vegetables grown God's way and man's way. Here is just one small example from that report. Snap beans grown organically had 60.00

grams of Magnesium. The inorganic had 14.8. Now you know why your mother told you to take your nutritional supplements. Be happy—the only one my mom knew about was Cod Liver Oil!

Then there is Noah's Ark. According to Ralph Muncaster, the detailed design of the ark of Noah is an example of an engineering design far ahead of its time. Naval engineers now know that the length-to-width ratio specified in the Bible in Genesis 6:15 is ideal for the stability of a barge-type craft designed for rough seas. It was not until the 1900's that comparably sized ships were constructed. Details of construction—including the waterproofing, room and deck structure, and the design of the

> *The God who made the world and everything in it is the Lord of heaven and earth.*
>
> *Acts 17:24*

opening for light—all display sound engineering.

If this subject fascinates you, there's more! All of these scientific theories were first mentioned by God in His Word:

- The fact that air has weight was addressed by Job when he wrote, "God . . . sees under the whole heaven; to establish the weight for the wind" (Job 28:24, 25). Scientists did not acknowledge this truth until Torricelli discovered barometric pressure in 1643. Until that time the scientific world believed that air was weightless.

- The first law of thermodynamics, which states that energy cannot be created or destroyed, was discovered by two scientists in 1842 but mentioned long before that by God in Hebrews

4:3, 4. "His . . . work has been finished since the creation of the world."

* The second law of thermodynamics, defined by Clausius in 1850, states that things tend to decay over time. The Bible declares in Isaiah 51:6, "The earth will wear out like a garment." Does this frighten you? It shouldn't because God's reliable Word also declares, "But in keeping with His promise we are looking forward to a new heaven and a new earth, the home of righteousness" (2 Peter 3:13). How soon will this happen? Not to worry! The Bible teaches that we will live in glorified bodies for a thousand years on this earth after Jesus returns. Is this difficult for you to believe? It shouldn't be, considering how fool-proof we are finding His Word to be. He has left us many awesome proofs of His creative power, wisdom, and knowledge.

Here is what seems like a far-fetched and difficult story to believe. The book of Exodus paints the picture of a very unhappy, grumbling group of people traveling from Egypt, the land of their captivity, to Canaan. Group? There were well over a million of them! They may not have missed the slavery they had endured, but they surely did miss the food! Here's what they said to Moses:

> *If only we had died by the Lord's hand in Egypt! There we sat around pots of meat and ate all the food we wanted, but you have brought us out into this desert to starve this entire assembly to death.*
>
> Exodus 16:3

It seems they were willing to be slaves for the food they loved.

God Himself had been providing food that miraculously appeared every morning. They called it "manna," meaning "What is it?" This alone may be enough to make a Bible skeptic laugh out loud. Look what comes next. In response to their incessant complaining about their boring diet, we read that God sent quail flying low enough for this group of "refugees" (remember, a million of them) to be able to simply reach up and grab their supper. Fairy tale? Myth? Impossible?

Here is a quote from the March-April 2002 paper, *Dispatch from Jerusalem* written by Haim Shapiro: "Quail is hardly a new item in the Jewish kitchen. According to the Bible, the Children of Israel ate quail in the Wilderness on their way from Egypt to the Promised Land. The wind carried the exhausted birds, which fell to the ground. In fact, residents of northern Sinai *still catch quail in nets as they fall to the ground on their annual migration northward.*" It wasn't such a far-fetched story after all!

About twenty-five years ago I wrote a filmstrip published by Child Evangelism Fellowship. It was called *Search for the Stars*. It showed in a rather comical way how, down through the ages, mankind has tried to discover answers about our universe. They could have saved themselves a lot of time if they had first consulted the Bible. Here is a condensation from the audio portion of that filmstrip:

This is Hipparcus, a scientist who lived over 2,000 years ago. Hipparcus was interested in astronomy, the study of the stars. "Now let me see, uh, 1,023, 1,024, 1,025. Yes, there are exactly 1,026 stars in the universe!"

Several hundred years later in the city of Rome lived Ptolemy, who also spent much time studying the stars. He said, "There are not just 1,026 stars in the universe, I've counted them, and there are 1,056 stars!" Everyone knew he was a great scientist, so everyone now believed that there were 1,056 stars.

But wait! A few years later there came along an even greater scientist named Galileo. Surely he would be able to tell us exactly how many stars there are in the universe. For you see, he had something to help him. He used a telescope to look up into the heavens. "Hold everything! With this telescope it is easy to tell that there are more than 1,056 stars in the universe. In fact, there are many other marvelous wonders to see when you *search for the stars.*"

Ever since Galileo counted the stars 360 years ago, men have been making larger and better telescopes and finding more and more stars. In fact, the 200-inch telescope has shown that there are billions of galaxies or groups of stars. . . .

Twenty-five years ago when I wrote that little cartoon filmstrip for children, the Hubble Telescope, which revealed an even larger universe, had not yet been built. There is nothing wrong with building bigger and better telescopes. They will only prove that, as God said in Jeremiah 33:22, the stars of the sky are *countless*! In Psalm 147:4 He tells us that He calls each star by name. Best of all, He knows your name, and He cares about you!

He also cares about Israel, as we shall see in our next chapter.

Chapter Four

Israel in Prophecy

If you were to ask me to tell you in just one word why I believe the Bible is the Word of God, I would say "ISRAEL!" Think about it. What land was given by God to the Jewish nation? ISRAEL! What land did God say the Jews would be driven out of if they did not obey His Word? ISRAEL! What one tiny country is mentioned every day on the news? ISRAEL! What country whose inhabitants, driven out for 2,000 years, came back home and are speaking their original language? ISRAEL! Why are these facts significant?

Israel is the only parcel of property on the globe given by God to a specific group of people. Surely God may have led some of my ancestors to the Ukraine and others to the Netherlands, but He specifically gave Israel to the Jews. The Bible declared in Genesis 15:18, "In the same day the Lord made a covenant with Abram, saying, 'Unto thy seed have I given this land, from the river of Egypt unto the great river, the river Euphrates.'"

We have, and rightly should have, a love for the Arab people. These are the children of Abraham by Hagar. But, these are not the people to whom God gave the land of Israel. Many people are not happy when they gather with their family members to hear their natural father's last *will and testament*. But the will stands. Our Heavenly Father's *will* is for Abraham's descendents, born through Isaac, to live in Israel. It is written in the Old Testament. It is His *will*! No matter how bad the situation seems for Israel, in the end, God's *will and testament* shall be executed.

Was God cruel to allow the Jewish people to be driven out of their land in A.D. 70? Let me answer this by asking another question. If your child constantly disobeys you by run-ning into the street to retrieve his ball when you have warned him that he must ask

> *Pray for the peace*
> *of Jerusalem*
> *Psalm 122:6*

you to get the ball for him, would it be cruel for you to take that ball away from your child? The laws given by God through Moses were for the protection and the good of the people. In Deuteronomy 30:19, God said, "… I have set before you life and death, blessings and curses. Now choose life. . . ." But they did not. The Bible declares in Deuteronomy 28:53-66, ". . . if you do not carefully follow all the words of this law . . . you will be uprooted from the land you are entering to possess. Then the Lord will scatter you among all nations, from one end of the earth to the other."

The great missionary and Bible teacher, Lester Sumrall, told this story: He was traveling deep in the jungles of South America where there were no roads and few people. He came upon a shack with a sign on the front indicating it was a store, so he went in. Inside he found that it was sparsely stocked with a few canned goods. Behind the counter he saw a man with a yarmulke on the back of his head reading the Hebrew Scriptures. The missionary asked the Jewish man, "What in the world are you doing here?" The gentleman responded, "Waiting to sell you something!" When the Romans came into Israel and drove these people out of their land, they were indeed scattered from one end of the earth to the other!

Hebrew, which until recent years was considered a dead language, is spoken in Israel today. We had a professor in college who had a doctorate in "dead" languages. Hebrew was one of them. The Bible declares in Zephaniah 3:9, "For then will I turn to the people a pure language, that they may all call upon the name of the LORD, to serve Him with one consent."

In 1881, Eliezer Ben-Yehuda moved with his wife to Jerusalem after hearing an inner voice saying, "Rebirth of Israel in the land of their forefathers." At that time Israel was under Ottoman control. Eliezer worked 18 hours a day for 41 years to bring to life that "dead" language. He determined to raise the first Hebrew-speaking children in 1,700 years, and when Ben Zion, his first child, was born, he forbade anyone to speak a word to him other than in Hebrew.

My dad's parents came to the United States from the Ukraine as newlyweds. My dad learned just a few Ukrainian words from them but could not speak or understand the language well enough to converse. I learned from my dad the four words in Ukrainian for "give me a kiss." I couldn't write it here because I don't know how to write these words and am not quite certain I pronounce them correctly. Yet, after almost 2,000 years of being scattered "from one end of the earth to another," the Jewish people are speaking the language of their forefathers—another amazing fulfillment of prophecy! Only God's prophecies are 100 percent correct all the time! (Did you know that Jacqueline Kennedy married Onasis one day after Jean Dixon "prophesied" that she would never re-marry?)

Try to find a newspaper, news magazine, or television news report that does not include the word ISRAEL, a country barely the size of the state of New Jersey. The impact of the Jews on our world is out of proportion to the size of their population. They are less than half of one percent of the people of the earth. Yet they have won 12 percent of the

Nobel prizes in chemistry, physics, and medicine. Amazing. They truly are God's chosen people. So, why are they so much in the news? It is not because of these accomplishments.

God Himself is directing our attention toward this tiny nation. He told Abraham that through his offspring all the nations of the earth would be blessed. Through these people we have received this awesome book, the Holy Bible, and through this nation we received our Savior. Yes, Israel as a nation sinned against God and was scattered, but He brought them back to their land. We who make up the nations of the world have sinned against God, but He gave us a way back to Himself through Jesus Christ. The Bible says in Romans 3:23, "For all have sinned and come short of the glory of God." It is God's intention to bring us all back to the birthplace of our salvation. Jeremiah 3:14, speaking of Israel says, "Return, faithless people . . . I will choose you—one from a town and two from a clan—and bring you to Zion." He has done this. He will surely do what follows:

> *At that time they will call Jerusalem the Throne of the Lord, and all nations will gather in Jerusalem to honor the name of the Lord. No longer will they follow the stubbornness of their evil hearts.*
> Jeremiah 3:17

When will these verses be fulfilled? We do not know God's timetable, but we do know that He seems to be focusing our attention on Israel at this point in history. Will you and I see this happen? Perhaps. Think about this: The order of events seems to be that God had to, against all odds, gather the Jews from every nation where He had scattered them. He would somehow focus the attention of the nations of the earth on Israel because we read in Revelation 1:7, "Look, He is coming with the clouds and every eye will see Him. . . ."

I find it interesting that the same generation of people who are alive to see Israel gathered back to her homeland is the same generation that has television. How else could "every eye" see him? People around the world saw the Twin Towers hit on September 11, 2001. Will something truly major be happening in Israel on the day when Jesus' feet touch the Mount of Olives so that our eyes are "glued" to our television sets?

Do you find it difficult to believe that Jesus will actually return to earth and His feet stand on the Mount of Olives? The Bible says:

> *On that day His feet will stand on the Mount of Olives, east of Jerusalem, and the Mount of Olives will be split in two from east to west, forming a great valley, with half of the mountain moving north and half moving south.*
> Zechariah 14:4

Did you know that seismologists have found a fault running from east to west through the Mount of Olives? Could it be that God knew it would be difficult for skeptics to believe that Jesus Christ would return bodily to this earth, so He allowed this fault to be discovered to make it easier for us to trust His Word? "...the mount of Olives will be split in two from east to west..." (Zechariah 14:4).

Let's look at the first part of 2 Peter 3:9, which is talking about the Day of the Lord when Jesus' feet stand on the Mount of Olives. In the first part of this chapter, he is talking about scoffers who would come saying, "Where is this 'coming' He promised?" In verse eight we read, "But do not forget this one thing, dear friends: With the Lord a day is like a thousand years and a thousand years are like a day."

One of the most amazing fulfilled prophecies concerning Israel is found in Daniel 12:12: "Blessed is he that waits, and comes to the thousand three hundred and five and thirty days" (1,335 days). Now, keep in mind 2 Peter 3:8, where we read in the last paragraph that with the Lord a day is like 1,000 years and 1,000 years are like a day. Daniel, at the time of this prophecy, was living in Babylon (now Iraq), meaning he was on the lunar calendar. Fast-forward 1,335 years to Jerusalem, then under the control of the Turks, who were also on the lunar calendar. On December 9, 1917, which was 1335 on the lunar calendar, the Turks evacuated Jerusalem and ended their 400 year domination of God's Holy City! Coins minted in that year of liberation actually bear the Arabic date 1335 as a tangible testimony of the accuracy of God's Holy Word. Why do I believe the Bible is the Word of God? Because no other book on planet earth has such detailed fulfilled predictions. Only an omnipotent God could have known what was going to happen to Jerusalem 1,335 years in the future.

Are you wondering why the Turks, after being in control of Jerusalem for 400 years, left so suddenly? I'm so glad you asked! Here again is what appears to be another fulfilled prophecy. The prophet Isaiah in chapter 31 and verse 5 predicted, "As birds flying, so will the Lord of hosts defend Jerusalem; defending also He will deliver it; and passing over He will preserve it." The liberation of Jerusalem in 1917 was an important event on God's end-time calendar. It was time for Israel to be regathered into her promised land. On November 2, 1917, the British Foreign Secretary, Arthur Balfour, made the following declaration:

> His Majesty's government view with favour the establishment in Palestine of a national home for the Jewish people, and will use their

best endeavours to facilitate the achievement of this object.

The person chosen to carry out "the achievement of this object" was General Allenby. The Turks were determined to defend Jerusalem and fight for their right to be there. Concerned that Jerusalem would be destroyed by his artillery, Allenby knelt in his tent and prayed that God would make the battle unnecessary.

Assuming that the British forces would be using one of the newly developed tanks they had heard about, the Turks began to seal up every gate in the walls of Jerusalem. Believing that the entry to the East Gate was too steep for the tanks, they planned to open it for their own use. They must not have been aware that God in Ezekiel 43 and 44 declared that the East Gate shall not be opened until Messiah comes through it again.

Just before the Turks could open the East Gate, God protected this prophecy by using yet another new weapon of war called an airplane! What a surprise for the Turks! They had never seen an airplane. From the plane the British dropped a message that said, "Surrender the city," and it was signed "General Allenby." "Allenby" is very close to "Allah bey," meaning, in the Turkish language, "Son of God." In great fear, the Turks fled without a struggle and "as birds flying the Lord God did defend Jerusalem."

Liberating Jerusalem was just the first step. God would, just as He had promised, reunite His people and establish them in the land of Israel. He was very specific about when this would happen. Due to the rebelliousness of His people, this step took much longer then it should have.

In Leviticus 26:18 God taught His people that whenever they sinned against Him, they would be punished. But, He promised to give them time to repent. If they did not repent, the remainder of their punishment would be multiplied by seven. He said, "If after all this you will not listen to me, I will punish you for your sins seven times over."

God told His prophet in Ezekiel 4:3-6 to lie on his side for 430 days to signify the 430 years Israel would spend in exile for her sins. He went to great lengths to show that He was serious about His Word. Then, He prophesied through Jeremiah that the first 70 years of the 430 years Israel would be held captive by the Babylonians. You can read about this in Jeremiah 25:11 "This whole country will become a desolate wasteland, and these nations [Judah and surrounding lands] will serve the king of Babylon seventy years."

In 606 B.C. the Jewish people found themselves captives in Babylon just as their prophets had warned. Exactly 70 years later, in fulfillment of Jeremiah's prophecy, Cyrus the Great of Persia came along and offered to pay for the Jews to go back to Jerusalem. Only 50,000 devout Jews went back. The rest were too entrenched in the Babylonian lifestyle. God was not pleased!

Now let me quote Paul Meier in the appendix to his novel *The Third Millennium:* "Take 430 years of exile, subtract 70 years of warning, and multiply the remaining 360 years times 7, as Moses instructed in the Torah. You will get 2,520 prophetic years of 360 days each = 907,200 days from the day Cyrus made his decree to return to Jerusalem, which comes out to [*are you ready for a shock?*] May 14, 1948, the day Israel became a nation." Amazing!

Grant Jeffery, in his book *Armageddon Appointment with Destiny*, reminds us, concerning the above, to keep in mind that there is only one year between 1 B.C. and A.D. 1. Therefore, the end of Israel's worldwide captivity would occur after a total of 2,483.8 years had elapsed from the spring of 536 B.C.

The math is worked out in detail in Grant's book.

Please understand that no mere mortal could have seen, more than 2,500 years earlier, the exact day that Israel would become a nation. Only our Creator God could have known this. He loved us enough to communicate His love and power to us through His Word, the Holy Bible. Events are taking place in our world exactly as He foresaw millenniums ago. God is in control. He knows the end from the beginning. What an awesome God we have! What an awesome book this is!

Watch Israel— God's Time Clock!

Look at God's "time-clock." He gave, He scattered, He restored. The way I see it, that hour hand must be pushing midnight! But, when Jesus' disciples asked Him what would be the sign of His coming, He said, "Keep watch because you do not know the day or the hour."

We have been watching. We have seen how He brought the Jews back from every nation where they were scattered. He has given us much detail. For instance, God spoke to Israel in Isaiah 43:5, 6: "Do not be afraid, for I am with you; I will bring your children from the east and gather you from the west. I will say to the north, 'Give them up!'" For years Russia refused to let any Jewish people leave. The government would not give them visas. Once again God kept His Word, and the north did give up His people—almost 800,000 Jewish citizens have immigrated from Russia to Israel. He has restored their language so they could "serve Him with one consent." And now, as we watch the evening news, we see many nations gathered against Jerusalem, even as God's prophets foretold.

I want to be like the men of Issachar of whom God said in 1 Chronicles 12:32, ". . . they understood the times in which they were living." So I keep one eye on my Bible and the other on the news. I watch to see if what I am seeing is a fulfillment of prophecy.

Here's an example. The last week of June 2002, there was much talk in the news about a "fence" that is being built to protect Israel from Arab terrorists—one eye on the news. Ezekiel prophesied of a day when the people of Israel would be living in safety, in a land of "unwalled villages"—one eye on the Bible. Could it be that these electronic fences might bring a time of safety from terrorist attacks? Only time will tell. Just as with the other prophecies we have already seen fulfilled, in God's time we will know if this also applies.

If you care to join me in watching for signs of Jesus' return, you might find Revelation 16:12 interesting: ". . . the great river Euphrates, and its water was dried up to prepare the way for the kings from the East." In 1973 a huge dam was constructed in northeast Syria on the

Euphrates River. Two more followed, one in Turkey and one in Iraq. Imagine how the Apostle John, who wrote the book of Revelation, must have felt when God showed him the great Euphrates River dried up and the armies of the east marching on dry ground toward Jerusalem! He must have thought, "Impossible!" But we have actually seen pictures of the dams! God is confirming His Word in our lifetime! Keep one eye on the news—your other eye on God's Word.

❦

Chapter Five

Prophecies Concerning Jesus

$\mathcal{M}$any years ago Henry Bosch wrote:

Socrates taught for forty years,
Plato for fifty, Aristotle for forty,
and Jesus for only three. Yet the
influence of Christ's three-year
ministry infinitely transcends the
impact left by the combined 130
years of teaching from these men
who were among the greatest
philosophers of all antiquity. Jesus
painted no pictures; yet, some of
the finest paintings of Raphael,
Michelangelo, and Leonardo da
Vinci received their inspiration
from Him. Jesus wrote no poetry;

but Dante, Milton, and scores of the world's greatest poets were inspired by Him. Jesus composed no music; still Haydn, Handel, Beethoven, Bach, and Mendelssohn reached their highest perfection of melody in the hymns, symphonies, and oratorios they composed in His praise. Every sphere of human greatness has been enriched by this humble carpenter of Nazareth.

Perhaps Henry Bosch was inspired by Forman Linicome, who wrote:

In infancy He startled a king, in boyhood He puzzled doctors, in manhood He walked upon the billows and hushed the sea to sleep. He healed the multitudes without medicine and made no charge for His services. He never wrote a book, yet not all the libraries of the country could hold the books that could be written about Him. He never wrote a song, yet He has furnished the theme of more songs than all song writers combined. He never founded a college, yet all the schools together cannot boast of as many students as He has. Great men have come and gone yet He lives on. Death could not destroy Him, the grave could not hold Him. We shall be forever with Him or without Him.

These thoughts are a reminder to us that literally millions of people throughout history have worshiped, written about, and laid down their lives for Jesus the Son of God. Yet, the Jews did not recognize Jesus as their Messiah. How could this be? There were over 300 prophecies in the Old Testament telling them what to look for. Were they not reading their own Scriptures?

I see two major reasons why they did not recognize their Messiah. One, unless the prophecies are studied very carefully, they are confusing. For example: Jesus would be born in Bethlehem, come out of Egypt, be called a Nazarene, and be a king with no place to lay His head. This does sound confusing, yet all of these prophecies were perfectly ful-filled. The New Testament teaches that God allowed the Jewish people to be confused or "blinded" for a time so that the Gentiles might be included

ॐॐ

He came to die on a cross of wood—yet He made the hill on which it stood.

in His plan of redemption. For this I am eternally grateful. But, keep in mind that the Jewish nation gave us our Jewish Messiah and Savior. They are still God's chosen race, and Scripture tells us, ". . . in a day all of Israel shall be saved."

And I will pour out on the house of David and the inhabitants of Jerusalem a spirit of grace . . . they will look on Me, the one they have pierced . . . They will call on My name and I will answer them; I will say, "They are My people," and they will say, "The LORD is our God."

Zechariah 12:10, 13

The other reason Jesus was not recognized as the Messiah of Israel had to do with the political situation the Jewish people were facing at the time of Jesus' birth. They were under Roman rule. They wanted to be free of this domination. Old Testament Messianic prophecies painted a picture of Jesus as a conquering king *and* a suffering servant. They were looking for the conquering king—certainly not the suffering servant. He came the first time "lowly and riding on a donkey." He will come the next time on a white horse as King of kings and Lord of Lords! Israel was looking for someone who could save them from Roman rule. Instead, He came to save us from eternal separation from God.

"Lowly (or gentle) and riding on a donkey." Let's take a look at this Old Testament prophecy and its fulfillment. See if you can see why the Jews were confused. It's found in Zechariah 9:9:

Rejoice greatly, O Daughter of Zion! Shout, Daughter of Jerusalem! See, your king comes to you, righteous and having salvation, gentle and riding on a donkey, on a colt, the foal of a donkey.

Now look at the fulfillment in Matthew 21:1-4:

As they approached Jerusalem and came to Bethphage on the Mount of Olives, Jesus sent two disciples, saying to them, "Go to the village ahead of you, and at once you will find a donkey tied there, with her colt by her. Untie them and bring them to me. If anyone says anything to you, tell him that the Lord needs them, and He will send them right away." We are now up to verse four which reads, *"This took place to fulfill what was spoken through the prophet: 'Say to the Daughter of Zion, "See, your king comes to you, gentle and riding on a donkey."'"*

Your *king*? But He was not king over Israel. The Romans ruled. He was not dressed like a king, and His transportation surely was not befitting a king! Yet, there were those who did recognize Him as their king, and they spread their cloaks and cut branches from the trees spreading them on the road ahead of Him and shouting, "Hosanna to the Son of David" and "Blessed is He who comes in the name of the Lord!" Others at the same time asked, "Who is this?"

This is not as difficult to understand as it at first appears. Daniel is saying that someday a decree will be made to rebuild the walls of Jerusalem. He also said that sixty-nine prophetic "weeks" after that decree, the Messiah would be recognized as "most holy." In his book, *The Third Millennium,* Dr. Paul Meier explains that the prophetic week has always meant seven 360-day Hebrew years. So, 69 "weeks" equals 69x7=483 years x 360 days=173,880 days. Any Jew could have done the math and shown up at the Eastern Gate on April 6, A.D. 32 to celebrate Jesus' triumphal entry. Perhaps the multitudes that gathered there on that day had simply done the math!

> *For he was cut off from the land of the living: for the transgression of my people he was stricken.*
>
> *Isaiah 53:8*

The Old Testament prophecies concerning Jesus included His genealogy, where He would be born, miracles He would perform, and others including why and how He would die. One interesting prophecy is found in Psalm 22, which accurately describes crucifixion. This is noteworthy because up until the time this psalm was written, crucifixion had not been practiced. It was popularized by the Romans about the beginning of the Christian era. Yet the psalmist wrote:

> *I am poured out like water, and all my bones are out of joint . . . they have pierced my hands and my feet. I can count all my bones; people stare and gloat over me. They divide my garments among them and cast lots for my clothing.*
>
> Psalm 22:14, 16, 17, 18

Our Father God, who knows the end from the beginning, looked down the corridors of time and saw the price His only Son would pay for our sins. This cross is seen in many places throughout the Old Testament as when Moses lifted up the serpent in the wilderness to bring healing to the children of Israel. This is the symbol used by the medical profession. I was interested to see that one of my former medical doctors had this symbol on his tie clasp.

Bible teacher Chuck Missler has found the symbol of the cross in a most unusual place. In Numbers chapter one, a seemingly boring text where the tribes of Israel were being numbered, Chuck asks, "Why did the Holy Spirit want you to know this list of numbers?" Good question. You will be able to understand the answer to this question if you can just picture with me God's instructions for encampment. The tabernacle of Moses was at the center of the camp of Israel. The tribe of Levi encamped around it. The three families of the tribe of Levi camped on the north, south, and west side of the tabernacle. The remaining twelve tribes were grouped into four camps around the Levites specifically assigned to the north, south, east, or west. If you tally the size of each tribe as they stretched out in each of the four directions, it will appear to be the form of a cross! (See illustration on the following page.) We were on His mind back then. We are on His mind now.

Since the Garden of Eden, mankind has refused to obey God's Word. Yet, His love for us and His plan to redeem us can be seen throughout the Bible, including the Old Testament.

The New Testament is in the Old concealed.

The Old Testament is in the New, revealed.

Is this difficult to understand? Yes, it is! Did you ever ask your mother a question and she replied, "Just because I said so?" Mom's word was law! So is God's Word. If a child does not understand the reasoning behind Mom's answer, her reasoning is not invalid. I remember declaring that I would never

The Camp o f Israel

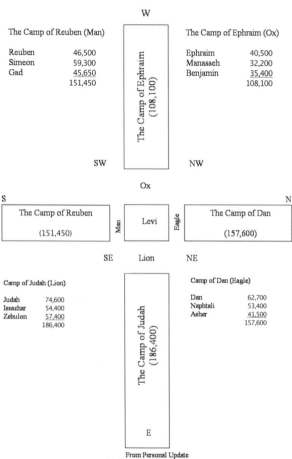

W

The Camp of Reuben (Man)

Reuben	46,500
Simeon	59,300
Gad	45,650
	151,450

The Camp of Ephraim (Ox)

Ephraim	40,500
Manasseh	32,200
Benjamin	35,400
	108,100

The Camp of Ephraim
(108,100)

SW   NW

Ox

S   N

| The Camp of Reuben | Levi | The Camp of Dan |
| (151,450) | | (157,600) |

Man   Eagle

SE   Lion   NE

Camp of Judah (Lion)

Judah	74,600
Issachar	54,400
Zebulon	57,400
	186,400

Camp of Dan (Eagle)

Dan	62,700
Naphtali	53,400
Asher	41,500
	157,600

The Camp of Judah
(186,400)

E

From Personal Update
The Newsletter of Koinonia House
Chuck Missler
February 1993

say, "Just because I said so," to my own children. But, there were times when I knew they were too immature to understand and so, horror of horrors, I did speak those words! My children's respect for me created an unspoken acceptance between us. My respect for God has come through my daily walk with Him at the center of my life and through the study of His Word. But, IF I COULD UNDERSTAND GOD COMPLETELY, I WOULD BE GOD. Who am I that I feel that I should be able to comprehend the everywhere present, all-powerful creator of the universe? As a child, it was comforting to me to know that my parents did know

The New is in the Old concealed. The Old is in the New revealed.

more than I did and that they had everything under control. Now that I am an adult, I am equally thankful that, during difficult times in my life, my Father God has everything under control.

With those thoughts in mind, let's think about the event that restarted the calendars of the world: the resurrection of Christ from the dead. King David of Israel prophesied in Psalm 16:10 that Jesus would be resurrected from the grave. ". . . you will not abandon me to the grave, nor will you let your Holy One see decay."

D.J. Kennedy, in his book *Why I Believe,* says, "I have met many people who do not believe in the resurrection of Christ, but I have never met one person who has read even a single book on the evidences for the resurrection who did not believe it." So, if you find it difficult to believe that Jesus Christ was resurrected from the grave, I would like to point you to a book we have had in our library for many years, *Who Moved the Stone?* by Frank Morrison. Morrison was a lawyer who wanted to write a book against the resurrection of Jesus. His first chapter was entitled "The Book That Refused to Be Written" because in his research in preparation for writing, he found the evidence so overwhelming that he became a believer. Likewise, Stan Telchin, also a lawyer, took a year off from his practice to disprove the claims of Christ because he was devastated when his daughter came to believe that Jesus was the Messiah of Israel. This Jewish lawyer's scholarly research resulted in his own quest for his Messiah and his book *Betrayed.* (Keep in mind that most early believers were Jews.)

Morrison gives us some interesting food for thought. He observed that there were only three groups of people who might have taken the body of Jesus: the Romans, the Jews, or the disciples. The Romans were interested in keeping the provinces quiet. Stealing the body of Jesus would not have benefited them. The Jews, in general, did not believe this humble Nazarene was their Messiah and asked that the tomb be guarded so that the believers could not steal the body. The third group, the disciples certainly had no reason to steal the body. So, who was left to steal the body of Jesus?

Think further about the disciples of Jesus. All but John suffered a terrible martyr's death such as being skinned alive or being crucified upside down. If they had taken the body and hidden it somewhere, wouldn't they have confessed and retrieved it before suffering in this way? Would they die for what they knew to be a lie? Yet secular and Christian history verifies the persecution the early Christians suffered for their faith in the resurrected Christ. It was the resurrection that turned the Apostle Peter from a "wimpy" guy willing to deny his faith in Jesus when confronted by a young girl into a fearless witness for Christ. He had seen Jesus in the upper room after His resurrection. So had hundreds of others who were willing to suffer persecution for their testimony. Today there are millions around the globe willing to be martyrs for Him because they have "seen" Him through the Bible. There were more martyrs for Christ in the twentieth century than in the preceding 1,900 years.

Throughout history people have sought to eradicate the witness of Christians. In A.D. 303 an edict was issued to destroy all of the world's Bibles. People found with Bibles were killed. In Nazi Germany people used to hide their Bibles in their flour bins. The agnostic, Ingersoll, held up a copy of the Bible and said, "In fifteen years I'll have this book in the morgue." Fifteen years rolled by, Ingersoll was in the morgue, and the Bible lived on. Voltaire said that in one hundred years the Bible would be an outmoded and forgotten book, to be found only in museums. When the one hundred years were up, Voltaire's house was owned and used by the Geneva Bible Society. And recently, ninety-two volumes of Voltaire's works were sold for two dollars (E.M. Harrison). God's Word lives on as a testimony of the resurrected Christ.

∂∞∞∂

Chapter Six

Changed Lives

ℐ have listed several reasons why I believe that the Bible is the inspired Word of God. But, what difference does believing that the Bible is the Word of God make in a person's life? In my introduction I mentioned that it gave me the assurance that I would see my mother again. That's good, but is that all?

Throughout the Old Testament you will observe that the nations that had a reverence for God prospered and were blessed. We read earlier that God gave Israel a forty-year period to repent when she wandered away from His principles. America is a good example. Someone once said, "America is great because America is good. When America ceases to be good, she will cease to be great." America was founded by people who came here because of their belief in the Bible. Our Founding Fathers set up our judicial, legislative, and executive branches of government according to Isaiah 33:22: ". . . the LORD is our Judge, the Lord is our Lawgiver, the Lord is our King." Many of our great universities, including Yale and Harvard, were founded by theologians. Their goal was to teach Biblical principles. America has been a safe haven for the "scattered" Jews we wrote about in chapter four. God has blessed America because America has had a history of blessing God. A study can be made of the rise and fall of nations according to their reverence for God.

Belief in God's Word can change nations. It can also change people. Let me share with you an example of the difference a belief in the Holy Scriptures can make in individual lives: Max Jukes lived in the state of New York. He did not believe in Christian training. He married a girl of like character. From this union they had 1,026 descendants. Three hundred were sent to the penitentiary for an average of thirteen years each and 190 were public prostitutes. There were 100 drunkards, and the family cost the state of New York $1,200,000. They made no contribution to society.

But . . . Jonathan Edwards lived in the same state. He believed in Christian training. He married a girl of like character. From this union had come, at the time of this research, 729 descendants. Out of this family have come three hundred preachers, sixty-five college professors, thirteen university presidents, sixty authors of good books, three United States congressmen, and one vice president of the United States; and except for Aaron Burr, a grandson of Edwards who married a woman of questionable character, the family has not cost the state a single dollar.

In the New Testament we read about a man named Saul. Saul hated Christians and took great pleasure in seeing many of them executed. In the ninth chapter of Acts we read that he was:

> . . . *breathing out murderous threats against the Lord's disciples. He went to the high priest and asked him for letters to the synagogues in Damascus, so that if he found any there who belonged to the Way, [followers of Christ] whether men or women, he might take them as prisoners to Jerusalem.*

But, the day came when Saul met this Jesus whose disciples he was persecuting. He was taught by those who knew Jesus—those who had walked and talked with Him. He came to love Him as so many have down through the centuries. As a result of his commitment to Christ, he writes in 2 Corinthians 11:23-25 how he was imprisoned, flogged, exposed to death, five times received from the Jews forty lashes minus one, three times beaten with rods, once stoned, three times ship-wrecked. He then goes on to tell of other dangers he had experienced. This man Saul had been raised in a good Jewish family and was a respected member of the Sanhedrin, the highest judicial and ecclesiastical

> **
>
> *Therefore, if anyone is in Christ, he is a new creation.*
>
> *2 Corinthians 5:17*

council of the ancient Jewish nation, com-prised of from seventy to seventy-two members. They were an elite and scholar-ly group! Yet Paul gave all this up in order to follow Jesus. History tells us that he suffered martyrdom at the hands of the Romans. Would he have been willing to suffer as he did, leaving a comfortable lifestyle for a legend? No. Myths do not make martyrs! He knew that Jesus was indeed the Son of God, who came to die for the sins of the world and to unite mankind with God their creator. It became his goal in life to introduce as many people as possible to Jesus. Nothing else mattered to him. Saul was changed by the "Incomparable Christ"! His name was changed from Saul to Paul.

Here is another name change: Perhaps you remember reading in the paper or hearing on the news of the capture of the serial killer "Son of Sam." This man, David Berkowitz, now refers to himself as "Son of Hope." Here is his story:

May God bless everyone who is reading this message. My name is David Berkowitz, and I am a prison inmate who has been incarcerated for more than twenty-two years. I have been sentenced to prison for the rest of my life. I was the notorious murderer known as "Son of Sam." It was eleven years ago, when I was living in a cold and lonely prison cell, that God got hold of my life. Here is my story of hope.

Ever since I was a small child, my life seemed to be out of control. When I was in public school, I was so violent that a teacher had to grab me in a headlock and throw me out of his classroom. I was plagued with bouts of severe depression. Two years of weekly psychotherapy had no effect on my behavior.

Thoughts of suicide often came into my mind. My dad had me talk to a rabbi, teachers, and school counselors, but nothing worked.

When I was fourteen, my mother died. I had no siblings, so it was just my dad and me. He had to work ten hours a day, six days a week. We spent very little time together. I felt hopeless and became even more rebellious. My dad managed to push me through high school. The day I graduated I joined the Army. Even in the service I had trouble coping, though I did manage to finish my three-year enlistment.

I got out of the service in 1974 and found myself living alone in New York City. I was twenty-two, and the forces of Satan were becoming more and more evident in my life. I had always been fascinated with witchcraft, Satanism, and occult things since I was a child. I used to watch countless horror and Satan-type movies, some of which totally captivated my mind. I felt as if something was trying to take control of my life. I began to read the Satanic Bible and to practice occult rituals and incantations.

Eventually, I crossed that invisible line of no return. I began committing horrible crimes. Looking back, it was all an awful nightmare, and I would do anything if I could undo everything that happened. Six people lost their lives. Many others suffered at my hand. I am sorry for this.

In 1978 I was sentenced to 365 consecutive years, virtually burying me alive behind prison walls. Ten years into my prison sentence, when I was feeling despondent and without hope, another inmate introduced himself and began to tell me that Jesus Christ loved me and wanted to forgive me. Although I knew he meant well, I mocked him because I did not think that God would ever forgive me or that He would want anything to do with me. Still this man persisted and we became friends. His name was Rick, and we would walk the yard together. Little by little he would share with me about his life and what he believed Jesus had done for him. He kept reminding me that no matter what a person did, Christ stood ready to forgive if that individual would be willing to turn from the bad things he was doing and put his full faith and trust in Jesus Christ and what He did on the cross—dying for our sins. He gave me a Gideon Pocket Testament and asked me to read the Psalms. I did. Every night I would read from them. It was at this time the Lord was quietly melting my stone-cold heart.

One night I was reading Psalm 34. I came upon the 6th verse, which says, "This poor man cried, and the Lord heard him, and saved him from all his troubles." It was at this moment, in 1987, that I began to pour out my heart to God. Everything seemed to hit me at once—the guilt of what I had done and the disgust at what I had become. Late that night in my cold cell I got down on my knees and began to cry to Jesus Christ. I asked Jesus to forgive me for all my sins. I spent a good while on my knees praying to Him. When I got up, it felt as if a heavy but invisible chain that had been around me for so many years was broken. A peace flooded over me. I did not understand what was happening. In my heart I just knew that somehow my life was going to be different.

More than 16 years have gone by since I had that first talk with the Lord. So many good things have happened in my life since. Jesus Christ has allowed me to start an outreach ministry right here in the prison. I can pray with troubled men as we read our Bibles together. I have worked as the Chaplain's clerk and also have a letter-writing ministry. The Lord has also made ways for me to share with millions via TV programs such as <u>Inside Edition</u>. I have been able to share what God has done in my life as well as warn others about the dangers of involvement in the occult.

One of my favorite passages of Scripture is Romans 10:13, "For whosoever shall call upon the name of the Lord shall be saved." Here it is clear that God has no favorites. He rejects no one, but welcomes all who call upon Him." I am not sharing this message simply to tell you an interesting story. Rather I want you to taste the goodness of God in the life of a man who was once a Satan-worshiper and a murderer, to show you that Jesus Christ can bring about forgiveness, hope and change.

I have discovered that Christ is my answer and my hope. He broke the chains of sin, self-will, and depression that had me bound. He has turned me from a path leading to eternal damnation in the lake of fire to the blessed assurance of eternal life in heaven. God has miraculously transformed "Son of Sam" into "Son of Hope." He wants to perform the same kind of transformation in your heart and life today! Love in Christ, David Berkowitz.

David has now been incarcerated for more than twenty-five years. Was his conversion simply a ploy to gain favor with the parole board? No. David does not attend parole hearings. He does not believe he deserves to be paroled.

Was David's conversion genuine? Judge Alexander, former prison guard says, "Once, at Attica prison, I looked into his eyes and saw the darkest evil I have ever encountered. Not many people have ever scared me, but David scared me." Later, seeing David after he had come to faith in Christ, Judge Alexander said, "Once where I could only see darkness and demons, I could now see David was overflowing with rivers of living water. We currently have the most wonderful fellowship in Jesus Christ!"

ॐ

"There is more grace in God's heart than sin in our past."

I mailed David a copy of the manuscript for this book. I received a letter granting me permission to use his testimony here. He said,

You certainly have my permission to use my testimony in your publication. It is all for God's glory. Besides, it's not really my testimony. Rather it is the testimony of what Jesus Christ has done for me. So everything belongs to Him anyway.

By the time I finished reading his letter I knew I had found a new brother in Christ.

⊸⊷⊸

Conclusion

*W*hen I began writing this book, I called it *My Legacy*. I wanted my grandchildren to know what I believed and why. I wanted each grandchild to take these pages to college with him. I wanted to ask each one to read it at least once each year. Joseph asked his kids to carry his bones around for three hundred years! Why should my request seem unreasonable?

Legacy is defined as a gift by will, something received from an *ancestor* or *predecessor*. I shall, if Jesus does not return in my lifetime, become an *ancestor* to my children's children. I shall be a *predecessor* of your children and your children's children. Yes, I bequeath the words contained in this book to all of the above. But, why? Just so you know what I believe? No, I do it because I believe these words can affect your eternal destiny. God said in Deuteronomy 30:15, 16:

See, I set before you today life and prosperity, death and destruction. For I command you today to love the Lord your God, to walk in his ways, and to keep his commands, decrees and laws; then you will live and increase, and the Lord your God will bless you in the land you are entering to possess.

(In our case, that Promised Land is Heaven.) God continues in verses 19 and 20:

This day I call heaven and earth as witnesses against you that I have set before you life and death, blessings and curses. Now choose life, so that you and your children may live and that you may love the LORD your God, listen to His voice, and hold fast to Him. For the LORD is your life.

Why does anyone leave a legacy? A legacy assumes that what is left will somehow bless or make happy the person or persons receiving it. I want to leave my son and daughter, their children and their children's children, the same peace, comfort, and fullness of life that I have experienced in knowing the Lord Jesus Christ—God's legacy to me.

For God so loved the world that He gave His one and only Son, [His legacy to us] that whoever believes in Him shall not perish but have eternal life. For God did not send His Son into the world to condemn the world, but to save the world through Him. Whoever believes in Him is not condemned, but whoever does not believe stands condemned already because he has not believed in the name of God's one and only Son. This is the verdict: Light has come into the world, but men loved darkness instead of light because their deeds were evil. Everyone who does evil hates the light, and will not come into the light for fear that his deeds will be exposed. But whoever lives by the truth comes into the light, so that it may be seen plainly that what he has done has been done through God.

John 3:16-21

From these verses we see that the choice is ours. Does God send anyone to hell? No! The Bible specifically states that hell was created for the devil and his fallen angels. But, you have a choice. You may choose to spend eternity with God in Heaven or with Satan in Hell.

Does this seem unfair to you? Think about this. We are made in God's image. This means that He experiences the same emotions we do. For instance, we are told in

Ephesians 4:30 not to "grieve the Holy Spirit," so we know that God can feel grief. We know from reading John chapter 3 that God experiences the emotion of love. In fact, Scripture teaches us that He is love personified. Here is an interesting one:

> *As a father has compassion on his children, so the Lord has compassion on those who fear Him…the LORD'S love is with those who fear Him, and His righteousness with their children's children—with those who keep His covenant and remember to obey His precepts.*
>
> Psalm 103:13-18

"As a father" if you had a choice, would you rather your children were puppets or flesh and blood? If they were puppets, they would come when you pulled the right strings, do what you told them when you made them, and say, "I love you" on com-

mand. On their more rebellious days that might be preferred. But, anyone who has had a child spontaneously throw his arms around them and say from the heart "I love you" will know that a puppet could never take the place of a self-willed child.

God did not create us as puppets. We make the choice to love Him or reject Him. We make the choice to read or not to read the Scriptures, His love letters to us. We have already seen how in the first book of the Bible, He began showing His plan to redeem us. His love and concern for us, His children, are seen throughout the Scriptures. He wants us to love and obey Him just as we want our children to love and obey us. He longs for that from us just as we do from our children. We may choose to read and obey His Word. We may choose life or we may choose death—eternal separation from God. Choose life!

Do you have a problem with the concept of Father, Son, and Holy Spirit? If you read and understand the Hebrew Scriptures, this may trouble you. Go to Genesis 1:1 and notice the Hebrew pronouns where God says, "Let *us* make man in *our* image." He refers to Himself as plural. He is three in one. Think about an egg. Is the yolk egg? Is the white egg? Is the shell egg? The Father is God. Jesus is God. The Holy Spirit is God.

Do you know people who profess to believe the Bible but who live lives inconsistent with its teachings? In Titus 1:16 we see that God knew that there would be such people: "They claim to know God, but by their actions they deny Him." The French writer Pascal saw such people in his day. In *Pascal's Pensees* we read, "I say there are few true Christians, even as regards faith. There are many who believe but from superstition. There are many who do not believe solely from wickedness. Few are between the two." Do these people bother you? Would you let the existence of such people keep you from being an example of a true believer? Worse yet, would you let them keep you from making a decision to obey God's Word? Would you let them keep you from Heaven?

Jesus said, in John 14:6, 7, "I am the way, the truth, and the life; no man comes to the Father except through Me. If you really knew Me, you would know My Father as well." The Jewish people didn't realize that He was God manifested in the form of a simple Jewish carpenter. We have been able to see from our overview of the Bible that God sent His Son to shed His blood for the remission of our sins.

Always be prepared to give an answer to everyone who asks you to give the reason for the hope that you have.

1 Peter 3:15

Christ died for our sins. . . . He was buried. . . . He was raised on the third day according to the Scriptures. . . . He appeared to Cephas, then to the twelve. After that He appeared to more than five hundred. . . .

1 Corinthians 15:3-6

Without Christ in our lives there is a chasm that separates us from God and Heaven. We must receive Christ in order to go to Heaven. "But as many as received Him, to them He gave the right to become children of God, even to those who believe in His name" (John 1:12). You may, at this point, ritualistically say, "Jesus, I receive you," and promptly become someone who professes to believe but whose life is inconsistent with the teachings of God's Word. In Acts 20:21 we read, "I have declared to both Jews and Greeks that they must turn to God in repentance and have faith in our Lord Jesus."

To repent actually means to turn around and go the opposite way. My husband's uncle, L.L. Legters, demonstrated this by marching from his pulpit to the back of the church saying, "I'm going to hell, I'm going to hell, I'm going to hell." At the back of the church he reversed his direction stating on his way back to his starting point, "I'm going to heaven, I'm going to heaven, I'm going to heaven!" "That," said he, "is repentance!"

It would be wrong for God to forgive anyone whose mind was still set in rebellion against Him. No honest judge would pardon a criminal if he knew that this person planned to continue in his life of crime. The only condition upon which God can righteously forgive any sinner is if the supreme desire of that person has changed from selfish, self-centered, self-willed indulgence to a supreme desire to live in full obedience to God and His Word. Christ called this change of heart "being born again."

Receiving Christ involves turning to God from self, trusting Christ to come into our lives and to forgive our life of opposition to His ways. It is not just an emotional experience or giving intellectual assent. Mother Teresa speaks of "intense interior life." She said it well.

Would you like to experience an intense interior life? St. Augustine said, "There is a God-shaped hole in every man's heart." May I suggest a simple prayer to fill that void?

Father God, I thank you for sending Your Son Jesus Christ to pay the penalty for my sins. I thank You that He rose from the grave to give me eternal life. Forgive me for going my own way. I surrender my life and my future to you. Live Your life in me as You please. Change my heart and my desires. Give me a hunger to know You and Your Word and to live a life that pleases You.

Thank You, Father, for hearing and answering this prayer. In the name of Jesus I pray.

Perhaps you are not yet at the point of wanting to believe that the Bible is the inspired Word of God. It is difficult to accept information that challenges long-held philosophies. As Grant Jeffrey puts it in his book, *Signature of God*:

> Many individuals who have rejected God and the Bible have a huge "investment" in their declared position of rejection of the scriptures . . . because it requires them to think seriously about God and their responsibility to Him. They would have to abandon their previously held agnostic position to which they are emotionally and intellectually committed.

If you fit this picture, please study the books listed in the bibliography at the end of this book. The consequences are much too serious to let this happen to you.

What if I am wrong and the Bible is not the inspired Word of God? I have lost nothing. I have lived a wonderful life at peace with my conscience and my Creator. Even if there was no Heaven to gain or Hell to shun, I have lost nothing.

I know that my Redeemer lives.
Job 19:25

What if you are wrong in believing that the Bible is simply written by mortals? You have everything to lose! Think about it!

I leave you this legacy because:

I know that my Redeemer lives, and that in the end He will stand upon the earth. And after my skin has been destroyed, yet in my flesh I will see God; I myself will see Him with my own eyes—I and

not another. How my heart yearns with-
in me!

Job 19:25-27

If you know Him, *I'll see you here, there, or in*
the air:

Comfort one another with these
words:

For the Lord Himself will come down
from heaven, with a loud command, with
the voice of the archangel and with the
trumpet call of God, and the dead in
Christ will rise first. After that, we who
are still alive and are left will be caught
up together with them in the clouds to
meet the Lord in the air. And so we will
be with the Lord forever.

1 Thessalonians 4:16, 17

Phyllis Robinson

Bibliography

Chapter One

Alfred Jones, *Dictionary of Old Testament Proper Names.* Kregel Publications, 1990.

National Enquirer, January 7, 1975, pp. 24, 25.

Charles Mercer, *Alexander the Great.* New York: Harper & Row, 1962, p. 61.

D.J. Kennedy. *Why I Believe.* Word Publishing, 1980, pp. 18-21.

D.J. Kennedy, *Skeptics Answered.* Multnomah Books, 1997, pp. 41, 42.

Chapter Two

D.J. Kennedy, *Why I Believe.* Word Publishing, 1980, p.32.

Ralph Muncaster, *Is the Bible Really a Message from God?* Harvest House Publishers, p. 24.

Grant Jeffrey, *Signature of God.* Frontier Research Publications, 1996, pp. 78,79.

Chapter Three

Ralph Muncaster, *Science—Was the Bible Ahead of Its Time?* p. 18.

Patrick Glynn, *God: The Evidence.* quoted in *Making Your Faith Your Own.* by Teresa Turner Vining, InterVarsity Press, p. 42.

S.I. McMillen, *None of These Diseases.* Fleming H. Revell Company, 1975, p. 18.

USA Weekend, August 2000.

Haim Shapiro, *Dispatch from Jerusalem.* March/April, 2002.

Chapter Four

Paul Meier, *The Third Millennium,* Thomas Nelson Publishers, 1993. p. 304.

Grant Jeffrey, *Armageddon. Appointment with Destiny.* Bantam Books, 1990, pp. 40, 41.

Chapter Five

Henry Bosch, *Encyclopedia of 7700 Illustrations.* Assurance Publishers, 1979, p. 647.

Paul Meier, *The Third Millennium.* Thomas Nelson Publishers, 1993, p. 305.

Chuck Missler, *Personal Update.* Koinonia House, February 1993.

D.J. Kenndey, *Why I Believe.* Word Publishing, 1980, p. 107.

Frank Morrison, *Who Moved the Stone?* Faber and Faber, 1930, pp. 9-12.

Stan Telchin, *Betrayed.*

Chapter Six

David Berkowitz, *Son of Hope (Tract).* Moments with the Book, 1999.

Chapter Seven

Pascal, *Pascal's Pensees.* A Dutton Paperback pp. 74, 75.

Grant Jeffrey, *Signature of God.* Frontier Research Publications, 1996, p. 270.

Do you believe the Bible is the Word of God?
If your answer is YES, then, WHY?

God has said to us in I Peter 3:15 to always be ready to give an answer for our faith in His Word. Can you do this? Tough times will come. Is your confidence in His message to us strong enough to get you through these times? Before you look inside this cover; try to think of at least three convincing reasons why you believe that the Bible is inspired by God. If you can't, then this book is for you.

If your answer is,NO, then, WHY not?

Exactly what made you decide *not* to believe that the Bible is God-inspired? This little book may challenge you! Knowing what you believe about the Holy Bible is a matter of life and death.

Author Information

Phyllis Robinson is the author of *Great Ideas for Banquets*. She has written devotions for children in *Keys for Kids*, *The Family Devotions Bible*, and *The One Year Book of Family Devotions* plus several magazine articles and booklets. She is the wife of one, mother of two, and grandmother of seven!

How to Contact the Author

Additional copies of Why I Believe The Bible Is The Word Of God are available from:

Phyllis Robinson
P.O. Box 1022
Georgetown, TX 78627

Now available in Spanish, Braille and on CD.
Soon available in Amharic and Russian.

www.whyibelievebook.com

Author is available for speaking engagements and special meetings.